MILNER CRAFT SERIES

Cottage Garden Embroidery

Judy Newman

SALLY MILNER PUBLISHING

Published in 1996 by
Sally Milner Publishing Pty Ltd
RMB 54 Burra Road
Burra Creek NSW 2620 Australia

© Judy Newman, 1996

0Design and layout by Anna Warren
Photography by Andrew Elton
Stitch guide illustrated by David Collins

Thanks to Stephanie Simes and Winsome Watts who stitched
Sweet Flowers, Cottage Garden Basket and
The Garden Path.

Embroidery designs and styling by Judy Newman
Colour separation in Hong Kong
Printed in Singapore by Kyodo Printing

National Library of Australia
Cataloguing-in-Publication data:

Newman, Judy.
Cottage garden embroidery.

ISBN 1 86351 193 8.

1. Embroidery - Patterns. 2. Decoration and ornament -
Plant forms. I. Title. (Series : Milner craft series).

746.4404

Contents

INTRODUCTION   4

About cottage garden embroidery   4
About this book   5

GENERAL INSTRUCTIONS   8

Transferring designs   8
Materials for stitching   8
Needles   8
Preparation   9
Laundering   9
Make it yours   9

PROJECTS   10

1   Chatelaine   10
2   Sweet Flowers   14
3   The Cottage   17
4   The Garden Wall   19
5   Cottage Garden Basket   23
6   Sunshine Cushion   25
7   Cottage Heart   29
8   The Backyard   31
9   The Garden Path   35
10 The Vegetable Garden   38
11 Cottage Lavender Sachet   43
12 Cottage Scene   46

STITCH GUIDE   48

Introduction

ABOUT COTTAGE GARDEN EMBROIDERY

The garden has always been a rich source of inspiration for embroiderers. All kinds of gardens and flowers have been depicted in stitchery in different cultures across the face of the earth and throughout the centuries. But the style which seems to be treasured by many people today, and the style which I love most, is the cottage garden.

The image of the humble thatched cottage surrounded by a lavish flowering garden conjures up a time when lifestyles were simpler and the pace of living was much more gentle. It strikes a note of romance in those of us who cherish the sight of tall stands of hollyhocks, the cheery face of the sunflower and the gentle fall of foxglove blooms.

Although the occupants of the thatched cottages featured in classic chocolate-box scenes would no doubt have been concerned mainly with the basics of survival, they nevertheless found the time and energy to grow a profusion of flowers in the front garden, for no better reason than the sheer delight they gained from the colourful blooms. And the more humble, practical back garden, with its neat rows of vegetables and utilitarian potting shed, and enough space for some fruit trees and perhaps a henhouse or duck pen, still charms us today, and remains something many suburban gardeners long for.

Cottage gardens were favourite subjects for watercolourists in the eighteenth century and were popular in embroideries at the beginning of the 1900s. By the 1930s the cottage and its surrounding garden was one of the most popular images depicted in stitchery. Often at the centre of the garden was a woman in a long crinoline dress, known as Dolly Varden or 'the crinoline lady'. Although this romantic scene may have been far from the reality most stitchers encountered, it probably provided solace and a sense of comfort and peace, in much the same way as images of cottage gardens do today.

If you share my love for cottage garden scenes and embroidery, I am sure you will enjoy stitching these designs.

Pictured above and on the following page are several charming old embroidered pieces featuring cottage garden scenes. Some are stitched over printed designs, while others have been stitched freehand.

ABOUT THIS BOOK

Gardening and embroidery seem to go together; they both require an investment of time and patience, but the rewards are great and include the pleasure of watching something beautiful grow. You will notice that in my embroidery I have created gardens in which hollyhocks are the size of sunflowers, violets are as big as roses and flowers from all seasons bloom side by side. While this may disturb the purists, I find this little departure from reality one of the rewards to be had from embroidering a garden!

The designs are stitched using just one or two strands of thread, which produces a very fine result. The stitches used are basic ones which you will probably already know. As you stitch your embroidery, treat my designs as a starting point—add your own touches, change the colours to suit yourself and combine elements from one design with those of another. Soon you will develop your own style and be creating your own cottage garden scenes. All the designs are suitable for framing, although for this book, some have been made into pincushions and other small items that would make lovely gifts. This, too, is entirely your choice.

General Instructions

Transferring designs

Trace the design, shown actual size, from the page. Use this as your master copy. Described below are two transferring methods, both of which involve using a light source. These are the most suitable methods for transferring detailed designs to pale-coloured, light- or medium-weight fabric.

Using a Light Box

Place the design on the light box, face up. Place the fabric over it, right-side up. Using a sharp, soft lead pencil or a water-soluble marking pen, trace over the design.

Using a Window

Use a window in place of a light box. Tape the design onto the window, then tape the fabric over it. Transfer the design as above.

Materials for stitching

Choose natural materials such as linen or cotton. When working with one or two strands of thread, a closely woven fabric is needed. Heavy, loosely woven linens such as those used for cross stitch and other counted thread embroidery are not suitable for fine embroidery in which just one or two strands of thread are used. Good quality calico and homespuns are easy to work with and are inexpensive, but the ideal choice is a fine, evenly woven linen. Dress fabric stores often carry a good range of finely woven linen such as that used for shirts. It is a pleasure to stitch and will last for many years.

Needles

Use a crewel needle for all stitching, except when working bullions, grub roses or colonial knots. The size of the crewel needle is up to you, but it should be quite small in order to suit the fine fabric and stitching featured in these designs. Try a size 9 or 10 crewel (sometimes simply labelled 'embroidery') needle.

For bullion stitches, grub roses (which are groups of bullions) and colonial knots, use a straw needle (also known as a milliner's needle). These are long and fine, with a small eye. They are ideal for stitches where the needle has to be pulled through loops of thread as they allow this to be done without pushing the loops out of place.

It is also useful to have tapestry needles on hand. Use them when working with thick threads.

PREPARATION

Before you start stitching, make sure you have all the required thread colours for your chosen design. Wind the threads onto cardboard holders and mark each holder with the colour code. When you require a length of thread, make sure it is no longer than about 30 cm (12''). Threads become thinner as they are pulled through fabric, so if you work with long pieces, by the time you reach the end, the thread will have worn considerably.

Most of the stitches in my designs require only one or two strands. Remove these from the length, then wind the remaining strands back onto the thread holder for use next time.

LAUNDERING

After you have completed the stitching, you should always wash your embroidery to remove stains and oils from your hands (even if the embroidery doesn't look soiled). In lukewarm water, gently wash the fabric using mild laundry soap; avoid rubbing the stitching. Squeeze the water through and rinse well. Place right-side down on a clean towel and press with an iron until dry. Do not leave to dry slowly as colours could run.

MAKE IT YOURS

Personalise your embroidery! After all, it's all your own work, so make sure you sign it by stitching your initials in a fitting place, such as the bottom right-hand corner (and date it, too, if you like). Why not add little touches to personalise the design. If you are giving an embroidery to a friend as a gift, why not add something meaningful to the scene, such as a cat for cat lovers, or your friend's favourite flowers. Many of the designs feature verses or sayings which can be substituted as you desire.

Projects

1 Chatelaine

MATERIALS

20 cm (8'') square linen fabric
DMC six stranded threads in the following colours:
520 dark green,
3705 dark apricot, 523 silver green, 554 violet light, 327 antique violet
dark, 352 coral light
20 cm (8'') of 115 cm (45'') wide printed cotton fabric
crewel, straw and tapestry needles
polyester fibre filling
cardboard
small amount wool flannel
one gold bead
five large decorative brass beads
embroidery scissors

Finished size: pincushion — 9 cm x 7 cm (3½'' x 2¾''); chatelaine — 80 cm (32'') in length

PREPARATION

Transfer the design to the centre of the linen fabric following the instructions for transferring on page 6.

EMBROIDERY

Lettering: one strand of 520 in backstitch.
Hearts: two strands of 3705 in satin stitch.
Lavender, at left: one strand of 523 in lazy daisy stitch for leaves and in stem stitch for stems; one strand each of 554 and 327 together in the needle for flowers, working a bullion stitch for each bloom.
Orange flowers, at top left: one strand of 523 in stem stitch for stems; one strand of 3705 in buttonhole stitch (just two or three stitches) for flowers, with three colonial knots at the top for buds.

CHATELAINE
Popular in Victorian times, the verse 'When this you see, remember me' is used here on a chatelaine pincushion. The other elements of the chatelaine are needle book, thimble or thread bag, and scissors.

Hollyhocks, at right: one strand of 520 in buttonhole stitch for leaves, working stitches to a point at the centre of the leaf, and in straight stitch for stems. Flowers: one strand of 352, 327 or 554 for flowers, working one stalk of flowers using 352 and the others with 327 at the bottom and 554 at the top. Work flowers in buttonhole rounds until the top, where each flower tapers off to a small bloom of two or three buttonhole stitches. Then work colonial knots at the top of each stalk.

TO MAKE UP

Pincushion

Trim linen to 11 cm x 9 cm (4½'' x 3½''). Cut a same-size piece of printed fabric and place right sides together. Stitch around the edges using a 1 cm (½'') seam allowance and leaving an opening on one side. Turn right side out and fill with fibre; stitch opening closed. Using two strands of 523, stitch a button loop at the centre top edge.

Thimble bag

Cut a piece of cotton fabric 18 cm x 13 cm (7'' x 5''). Bring 13 cm (5'') edges right sides together; stitch using a 1 cm (½'') seam. Fold so that seam falls at centre back; stitch across bottom edge and neaten seams. Turn right side out and stitch a 2.5 cm (1'') hem at top edge of bag. Using six strands of 520 in a 25 cm (10'') length, threaded in a tapestry needle, work running stitches around the hem edge. Thread each end of the 520 thread through a brass bead and knot to keep the bead in place.

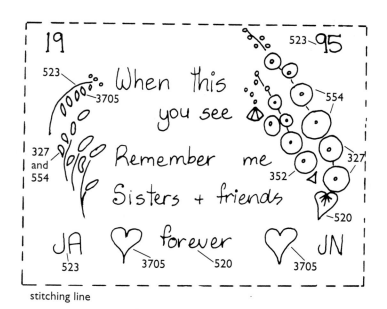

stitching line

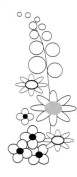

Needle book

Cut two 13 cm x 9 cm (5'' x 3½'') pieces of printed cotton. Place fabric right sides together and stitch around the edges, using a 1 cm (½'') seam allowance and leaving one short side open. Trim and turn right side out. Cut two 7 cm x 5 cm (2¾'' x 2'') pieces of cardboard and slip into the fabric to stiffen needle book covers. Turn the seam allowance on the open edge to the inside and slipstitch closed.

Using pinking shears, cut one 10 cm x 6 cm (4'' x 2½'') piece of flannel for the inside pages. Fold in half, bringing 6 cm (2½'') edges together and stitch into the centre of needle book by stitching centre fold of flannel to the spine line of book.

ASSEMBLY

Take a 1.8m (2 yd) length of six strands of 520 thread. Tape one end to your work table and make a twisted thread cord by twisting the other end until the thread is tightly ravelled. Pick up the thread in the centre and allow it to twist around itself.

Assemble the chatelaine by attaching the scissors, needle book, thimble bag and pincushion to the cord as desired, knotting brass beads at intervals between each item.

2 Sweet Flowers

MATERIALS

25 cm (10'') square piece of linen
DMC six stranded threads in the following colours:
3787 dark grey brown, 3346 hunter green, 3705 dark apricot, 3706 apricot,
3708 light apricot, 208 violet, 937 avocado green medium, 554 violet light,
726 topaz light
Crewel and straw needles

Finished size: embroidered area—9 cm (3½'') square

PREPARATION

Transfer the design to the centre of the linen fabric following the
instructions for transferring on page 6.

EMBROIDERY

Lettering and cottage: one strand of 3787 in backstitch; work door
handle with one colonial knot.

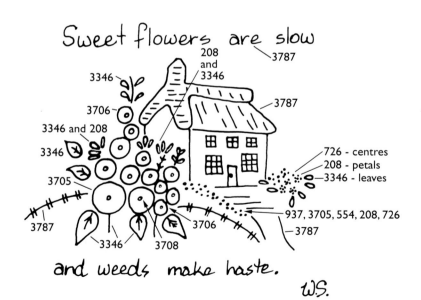

Fence: two strands of 3787 in backstitch, with posts formed by two parallel straight stitches.

Hollyhocks: one strand of 3346 in satin leaf stitch for leaves and in stem stitch for stems. Add a few lazy daisy stitches at the top of stems for small leaves. Flowers: one strand of 3705, 3706 or 3708 in buttonhole rounds, using colours as pictured (3705 on left stem at bottom, 3708 on centre stem and 3706 on top left and right stem). Using matching colours, work colonial knots in the centre of each flower.

Lavender: one strand each of 208 and 3346 together in the needle for flowers, working a bullion stitch for each bloom.

Knot flowers at right: one strand of 208 in colonial knots, making a group of four knots for each flower, then work a single 726 colonial knot in the centre of each group. Leaves: one strand of 3346 in lazy daisy stitch.

Knot flowers at left of path: either two strands of 937, two strands of 3705, two strands of 554, or one strand each of 208 and 726 in colonial knots, mixing the colours at random.

Frame as desired.

SWEET FLOWERS
A thatched cottage before a background of hollyhocks forms the centrepiece for a needle book. The quote is by William Shakespeare.

THE COTTAGE
This tiny design can be stitched quickly and is perfect for framing or for adorning a lavender sachet.

3 The Cottage

MATERIALS

20 cm (8") square linen fabric
DMC six stranded threads in the following colours:
844 beaver grey ultra dark, 520 dark green, 3731 rose, 304 crimson,
793 cornflower blue medium, 472 avocado green ultra light, 798 delft blue
dark, 988 forest green medium, 791 cornflower blue very dark, 208 violet,
ecru, 727 topaz very light, 840 beige brown medium, 895 christmas green
dark, 894 carnation very light, 776 pink medium, 917 plum medium
Crewel and straw needles

Finished size: embroidered area—6 cm (2½") square

PREPARATION

Transfer the design to the centre of the linen fabric following the
instructions for transferring on page 6.

EMBROIDERY

Cottage: one strand of 844 in backstitch for all except outline, which
should be worked in two strands of 844.

Garden from left

Hollyhocks: one strand of 520 in buttonhole stitch for leaves, working

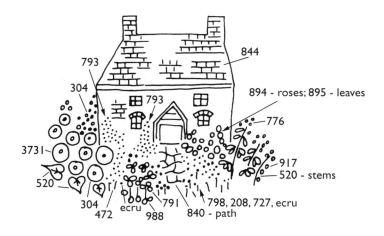

stitches to a point at the centre of the leaf, and in backstitch for stems.
Flowers (from left): one strand of 3731 in buttonhole rounds, gradually becoming smaller towards the top of the stalk, and finishing with three colonial knots at the top. Work remaining two stalks in the same way, using 304 thread, but adding more colonial knots at the top of the stalk.
Delphiniums: one strand of 793 in closely grouped colonial knots.
Bells of Ireland: one strand of 472 in closely grouped colonial knots.
Leaves at base of flowers: one strand of 988, using buttonhole stitches in groups of two or three to form leaves; work stems in straight stitch.
Flowers along path at left: one strand of 791 in groups of three lazy daisy stitches; fill any gaps with colonial knots of either one strand of 798, 208, ecru or 727, in groups of each colour.
Path: one strand of 840 in backstitch.
Flowers at right of path: one strand of ecru worked in groups of colonial knots; one strand of 798 worked in groups of three colonial knots, with a colonial knot centre of one strand of 727, to form forget-me-nots.
Roses: one strand of 895 in lazy daisy stitch for leaves; two strands of 894 in a colonial knot for each rosebud.
Foxgloves: one strand of 520 in stem stitch for stems; one strand of 776 in groups of two or three buttonhole stitches for foxglove flowers, adding colonial knots at the top of the stem for buds. Work two more foxgloves at right side using 917.

Frame as desired.

4 The Garden Wall

MATERIALS

25 cm x 20 cm (10'' x 8'') piece of linen fabric
DMC six stranded threads in the following colours:
640 beige grey very dark, 987 forest green dark, 351 coral, 742 tangerine light, 3371 black brown, 210 lavender medium, 726 topaz light, 3011 khaki green dark, 760 salmon, 793 cornflower blue medium, 327 antique violet dark
Crewel and straw needles

Finished size: embroidered area—10 cm x 7 cm (4'' x 2¾'')

PREPARATION

Transfer the design to the centre of the linen fabric following the instructions for transferring on page 6.

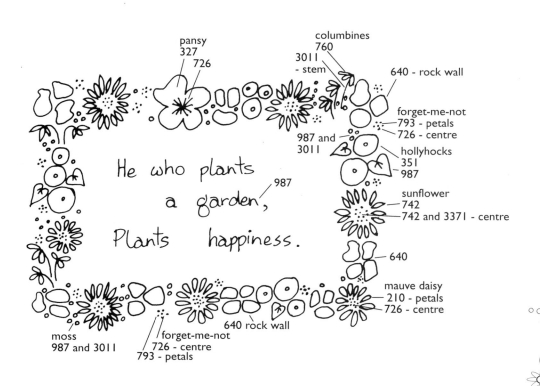

EMBROIDERY

First work the lettering and the rock wall. Then stitch the larger flowers: hollyhocks, sunflowers, daisies and columbines. Then work forget-me-nots and colonial knots for green moss to fill in the gaps.

Lettering: one strand of 987 in backstitch.

Rock wall: one strand of 640 in backstitch.

Hollyhocks: one strand of 987 in buttonhole stitch for leaves, working stitches to a point at the centre of the leaf; one strand of 351 in buttonhole rounds for flowers.

Sunflowers: one strand of 742 in lazy daisy stitch for petals; one strand each of 742 and 3371 together in the needle, worked in colonial knots for centres.

Mauve daisies: one strand of 210 in lazy daisy stitch for petals; one strand of 726 in colonial knots for centres.

Columbines: one strand of 3011 in stem stitch for stem; one strand of 760 worked in groups of three lazy daisy stitches for petals.

Pansy: one strand of 327 in satin stitch for outer petals, working from centre to outside edge; work centres in one strand of 726 in satin stitch.

Forget-me-nots: one strand of 793 in colonial knots, positioning together groups of four knots, with a single 726 colonial knot in the centre.

Moss: one strand each of 987 and 3011 together in the needle, worked in colonial knots, to fill gaps between flowers.

Frame as desired.

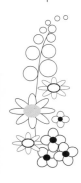

THE GARDEN WALL
An old Chinese proverb is surrounded by cottage blooms set amongst a
garden wall.

COTTAGE GARDEN BASKET

A profusion of blooms in a basket makes the prettiest of pictures. The basket is stitched in blocks of satin stitch, giving a dimensional feeling to the piece.

5 Cottage Garden Basket

MATERIALS

20 cm (8'') square linen fabric
DMC six stranded threads in the following colours:
372 beige, 3013 khaki green light, 208 violet, 726 topaz light, 987 forest green dark, 744 yellow pale, 971 pumpkin, 501 blue green dark, 3746 lilac, 917 plum medium, 798 delft blue dark, 792 cornflower blue dark, 793 cornflower blue medium, 524 silver green medium, 604 cranberry pink light, 3052 grey green medium, 420 hazelnut brown dark, 645 beaver grey very dark
Crewel and straw needles

Finished size: embroidered area—6 cm (2½'') square

PREPARATION

Transfer the design to the centre of the linen fabric following the instructions for transferring on page 6.

EMBROIDERY

Basket: one strand each of 372 and 3013 together in the needle, worked in straight stitch groups following the basket pattern. Outline the basket in stem stitch.

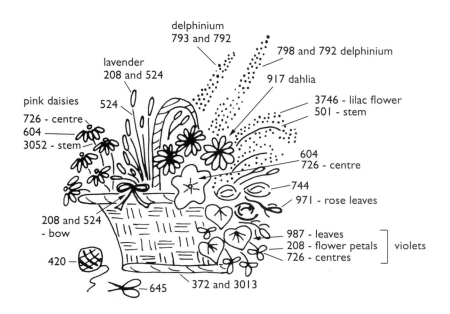

Violets: two strands of 208 in lazy daisy stitch, working three stitches for each flower; one strand of 726 in a single colonial knot to form the centre of each violet. Leaves: two strands of 987 in buttonhole stitch, shaped to form a point at the leaf centre.

Yellow roses: two strands of 744 in bullion stitches, worked in a grub rose formation; one strand of 744 in single bullions for rosebuds. Leaves: two strands of 971 in straight stitch.

Lilac: one strand of 501 in stem stitch for stems; two strands of 3746 in close groups of colonial knots for flowers, adding a few knots in 501 at the end of flower stems for leaves.

Dahlias: two strands of 917 in lazy daisy stitch.

Delphinium (on right): one strand each of 798 and 792 together in the needle, worked in colonial knots.

Delphinium: one strand each of 793 and 792 together in the needle, worked in colonial knots.

Lavender: one strand each of 208 and 524 together in the needle for flowers, worked in bullion stitch; two strands of 524 in stem stitch for stems. As well as the bunch of lavender at left of the basket handle, there are blooms scattered between other flowers to fill in gaps.

Pink daisies: two strands of 604 in lazy daisy stitch for petals; one strand of 726 in a single colonial knot for centres. Stems: two strands of 3052 in stem stitch.

Twine: one strand of 420 in small backstitches.

Scissors: one strand of 645 in small backstitches.

Bow on basket handle: one strand each of 208 and 524 are used to form a loose bow on the handle. With both threads together in the needle take a stitch through the fabric to secure the threads, leaving both ends free. Tie ends in a bow, then trim to desired length.

Frame as desired.

6 Sunshine Cushion

MATERIALS

25 cm x 22 cm (10'' x 9'') piece of homespun fabric
DMC six stranded threads in the following colours:
610 drab brown very dark, 937 avocado green medium, 3326 salmon pink,
988 forest green medium, 725 topaz, 741 tangerine medium, 886 leaf green,
3350 dusty rose very dark, 402 mahogany very light, 744 yellow pale,
335 rose, 894 carnation very light
Crewel and straw needles
30 cm (12'') of 115 cm (45'') wide cotton fabric, for cushion
Sewing thread

Finished size: embroidered area—12 cm x 9 cm (4¾'' x 3½'');
cushion centre—17 cm x 14 cm (6½'' x 5½'');
cushion—30 cm x 28 cm (12'' x 11'')

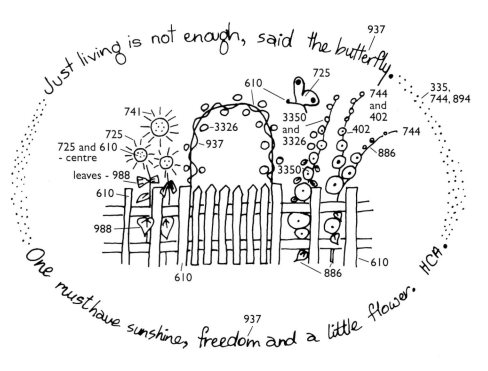

PREPARATION

Transfer the design to the centre of the homespun following the instructions for transferring on page 6.

EMBROIDERY

Fence, gate and arch: one strand of 610 in small backstitches.

Rose over arch: one strand of 937 in stem stitch for foliage; one strand of 3326 in bullion stitch for rosebuds, worked by placing three bullions beside each other.

Sunflowers: one strand of 988 in buttonhole stitches shaped to form a leaf; one strand of 725 in lazy daisy stitch for lower flower petals, worked closely together with some overlapping; one strand each of 725 and 610 together in the needle, worked in colonial knots for centres. Top sunflower: use 741 in place of 725.

Hollyhocks: one strand of 886 in buttonhole stitch shaped to form a leaf.

Flowers (stalk on the left): one strand of 3350 in buttonhole rounds, decreasing the size of the round as you work towards the top; work three colonial knots on top, using one strand each of 3350 and 3326 together in the needle; (centre stalk): work in the same way, using 402 for the main colour and using 744 and 402 together in the needle for the top; (right stalk): work in same way, using 744.

Lettering: one strand of 937 in small backstitches.

Knot flowers between lettering: one strand of either 335, 744 or 894 in colonial knots, mixing the colours at random.

Butterfly: one strand of 725 in satin stitch. Outline body with one strand of 610 in backstitch, with colonial knots for head and wing spots.

TO MAKE UP

Trim embroidery to 19 cm x 16 cm (7½'' x 6½'').

Cut two fabric strips 32 cm x 9 cm (13'' x 3½'') for top and bottom border, and two 16 cm x 8.5 cm (6½'' x 3¼'') strips for side borders. Stitch side borders in place using 1 cm (½'') seam allowance. Stitch top and bottom borders in place.

Cut two 30 cm x 20 cm (12'' x 8'') pieces for back sections. Hem one long edge on each piece. Overlap the two hemmed edges of the back pieces and place right sides together with the front, adjusting the positioning of the back pieces to fit the front. Stitch around cushion using 1 cm (½'') seam allowance; neaten seams. Turn right side out and press.

Embroidered text on cushion centre:
...but living is not enough, said the butterfly...
One must have sunshine, freedom and a little flower.

SUNSHINE CUSHION
A quote by Hans Christian Andersen is framed by joyous sunflowers, an arch of roses and tall stands of majestic hollyhocks to make this cushion centre.

COTTAGE HEART
Vividly coloured cottage garden blooms are celebrated in this heart, which wreaths a quote by Ralph Waldo Emerson.

COTTAGE SCENE
This design would look lovely on the edge of a handtowel or stitched as a border on a traycloth.

7 Cottage Heart

MATERIALS

30 cm (12") piece of linen fabric
DMC six stranded threads in the following colours:
600 cranberry very dark, 550 violet very dark, 553 violet medium,
743 yellow medium, ecru, 892 carnation medium, 341 hydrangea blue,
605 cranberry very light, 725 topaz, 727 topaz very light, 3731 rose,
561 emerald green, 798 delft blue dark, 742 tangerine light, 3371 black
brown
DMC Perle 5 thread: 3348 yellow green light
Crewel and straw needles

Finished size: embroidered area—13 cm x 9 cm (5" x 3½")

PREPARATION

Transfer the design to the centre of the linen fabric following the
instructions for transferring on page 6.

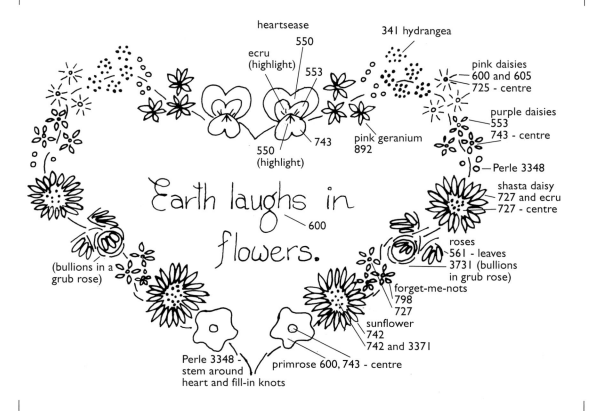

EMBROIDERY

Lettering: one strand of 600 in small backstitches, with colonial knots for the dots over the 'i' and the full point at end of the word 'flowers'. Work individual flowers from the top of the heart.

Heartsease: work in satin stitch, stitching from the outside edge of petals; one strand of 550 at outer edge of top petals; stitch next layer of colour using 553; stitch lower petals in one strand of 743. Work centre highlights using single strands of ecru and 550, referring to colour picture for placement.

Pink geraniums: two strands of 892 in lazy daisy stitch.

Hydrangeas: two strands of 341 in colonial knots, working in groups of seven or nine knots for each flower head.

Pink daisies: one strand each of 600 and 605 together in the needle, worked in straight stitches from the centre of the flower to the outside edge; one strand of 725 in colonial knots for centres.

Violets: one strand of 553 in lazy daisy stitch, working in groups of five for each flower; one strand of 743 in a single colonial knot for each centre.

Shasta daisy: one strand each of ecru and 727 together in the needle, worked in lazy daisy stitch for petals; work petals closely together, almost overlapping, and vary the lengths; one strand of 727 in colonial knots for centres.

Roses: two strands of 3731 in bullion stitches, arranged to form a large rose (grub rose), with two rosebuds at either side. Leaves: two strands of 561 in bullion stitch.

Forget-me-nots: one strand of 798 in lazy daisy stitch, working five for each flower; one strand of 727 in a single colonial knot for the centre.

Sunflowers: two strands of 742 in lazy daisy stitch for petals; one strand each of 742 and 3371 together in the needle, worked in colonial knots for centres.

Primroses: one strand of 600 in buttonhole stitch, working stitches to form the shape of petals by lengthening and shortening them; two strands of 743 in straight stitch for the centre, working from the centre to the outside edge.

Green stem around entire heart: one strand of 3348 Perle thread, working in stem and straight stitch between the flowers; work colonial knots in the same thread in groups to fill gaps below violets and amongst hydrangeas.

8 The Backyard

MATERIALS

25 cm x 20 cm (10" x 12") homespun fabric
DMC six stranded threads in the following colours:
840 beige brown medium, 3012 khaki green medium, 319 pistachio green
very dark, 3799 steel grey, 610 drab brown very dark, 3776 terracotta pale,
437 tan light, 975 golden brown dark, 937 avocado green medium,
471 avocado green very light, 988 forest green medium, 906 parrot green
medium, ecru, 886 leaf green, 498 christmas red dark, 739 tan ultra very
light, 792 cornflower blue dark, 832 olive green, 326 rose very deep,
893 carnation light, 600 cranberry very dark, 3825 pale peach,
3805 shocking pink, 3705 dark apricot
Crewel and straw needles

Finished size: embroidered area—12 cm x 8 cm (4¾" x 3")

PREPARATION

Transfer the design to the centre of the homespun following the
instructions for transferring on page 6.

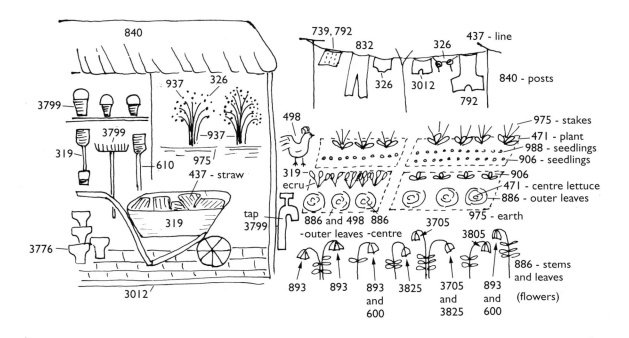

Shed: one strand of 840 in backstitch for roof and post; one strand of 3012 in backstitch for floor.

Tools

Wheelbarrow and spade: one strand of 319 in backstitch for outlines and in satin stitch for filled-in areas; two strands of 437 in blocks of satin stitch for straw in barrow.

Rake and buckets: one strand of 3799 in backstitch for outlines and in satin stitch for filled-in areas.

Shovel: one strand of 610 in backstitch for outlines and in satin stitch for filled-in areas.

Pots: one strand of 3776 in satin stitch.

Ground and stakes: one strand of 975 in straight stitch for areas under bushes and for stakes in vegetable garden and in running stitch for around garden.

Berry bushes: one strand of 937 in backstitch for stems and in colonial knots for leaves; one strand of 326 in colonial knots for berries.

Rooster: one strand of 498 in small backstitches.

Tap: two strands of 3799 in backstitch.

Vegetable garden

Seedlings at back: one strand of 471 in lazy daisy stitch.

Small seedlings: one strand of 988 (back row) and 906 (front row) in colonial knots.

Seedlings on right behind lettuce: one strand of 906 in lazy daisy stitch.

Spinach: one strand of ecru in straight stitch for stems; one strand of 319 in lazy daisy stitch for leaves.

Lettuce on right: two strands of 471 in bullion stitch for centre leaves; two strands of 886 in bullion stitch for outer leaves—all worked in a grub rose formation.

Mignonette lettuce on left: two strands of 886 in bullion stitch for centre; one strand each of 886 and 498 together in the needle for outer leaves.

Flowers at front: one strand of 886 in backstitch for stems and in lazy daisy stitch for leaves; use one strand of each thread for flowers, working each individual flower in colours as follows (from left to right): 893; 893; 893 and 600 together in the needle; 3825; 3705; 3705 and 3825 together in the needle; 3805; and 893 and 600 together in the needle. Work in a group of three buttonhole stitches for each flower cluster, working in such a direction that the flower faces downwards.

THE BACKYARD
A potting shed, garden tools, the vegetable patch and an old-fashioned washing line are all part of this charming backyard scene.

Washing line: two strands of 840 in backstitch for posts; one strand of 437 in backstitch for line.

Washing, from left

Cloth: two strands of 739 in satin stitch, with stripes of 792 stitched by weaving through the 739 stitching.
Pants: two strands of 832 in satin stitch.
Knickers: two strands of 326 in satin stitch.
Shorts: two strands of 3012 in satin stitch.
Bra: two strands of 326 in satin stitch, with details in backstitch.
Dress: two strands of 792 in satin stitch.

9 The Garden Path

MATERIALS

20 cm (8'') square homespun fabric
DMC six stranded threads in the following colours:
801 coffee brown dark, 434 brown light, 645 beaver grey very dark,
612 drab brown medium, 500 blue green very dark, 3364 pale moss,
744 yellow pale, 792 cornflower blue dark, 793 cornflower blue medium, 327
antique violet dark, 725 topaz, 962 dusty rose medium, 471 avocado green
very light, 931 antique blue medium, 824 blue very dark,
3688 mauve medium, 3041 antique violet medium, 924 grey green
very dark
Crewel and straw needles

Finished size: embroidered area—10 cm x 8 cm (4'' x 3'')

PREPARATION

Transfer the design to the centre of the homespun following the
instructions for transferring on page 6.

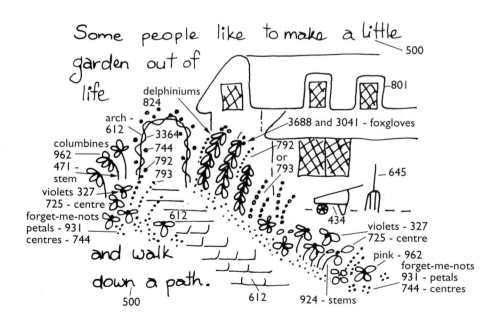

Some people like to make a little garden out of life

and walk down a path.

THE GARDEN PATH
An English-style cottage with stone pathway is bordered by a profusion of colourful cottage blooms. The quote is by Jean Anouilh.

EMBROIDERY

Cottage: one strand of 801 in small backstitches for outline of roof and walls and in straight stitch for outline of window panes.

Wheelbarrow: one strand of 434 in small backstitches.

Rake: one strand of 645 in small backstitches.

Steps, path and arch: one strand of 612 in close stem stitches for steps, in chain stitch for arch and in small backstitches for path.

Lettering: one strand of 500 in small backstitches.

Rose over archway: one strand of 3364 in straight and stem stitches to suggest stems and leaves; one strand of 744 in small bullion stitches for roses.

Flowers on left of path

Delphiniums: one strand of either 792 or 793, working in columns of colonial knots.

Violets: two strands of 327 in lazy daisy stitch, working three for each flower; one strand of 725 in a single colonial knot for centres.

Columbines (pink flowers at left of arch): two strands of 962 in lazy daisy stitch for flowers; two strands of 471 in stem stitch for stems.

Forget-me-nots: two strands of 931 in colonial knots, working four knots for each flower; one strand of 744 in a single colonial knot for each centre. Work forget-me-nots as fill-in flowers in gaps between larger blooms.

Delphiniums at right side: work as for delphiniums above, using 824 also for some blooms.

Foxgloves: two strands of either 3688 or 3041 (mix the colours), working in groups of three buttonhole stitches for each flower.

Fill right side of pathway by working pink flowers in 962 (as for columbines), forget-me-nots (colours as above) and violets (as above). Add stems in stem stitch using one strand of 924.

10 The Vegetable Garden

MATERIALS

30 cm (12'') square of beige linen fabric
DMC six stranded threads in the following colours:
844 beaver grey ultra dark, 934 black avocado green, 3799 steel grey,
3012 khaki green medium, 957 geranium pale, 210 lavender medium,
340 light mauve, 223 shell pink medium, ecru, 727 topaz very light,
320 pistachio green medium, 498 christmas red dark, 988 forest green
medium, 471 avocado green very light, 746 off white, 895 christmas green
dark, 502 blue green, 3348 yellow green light, 704 chartreuse bright,
740 tangerine, 924 grey green very dark, 370 beige gold, 321 christmas red,
919 red copper, 970 pumpkin light, 742 tangerine light
Crewel and straw needles

Finished size: embroidered area—12 cm (4¾'') square

THE VEGETABLE GARDEN

With its neat ordered rows of vegetables, this garden is every bit as charming as its showier cousin—the flower garden. Strawberries, seedlings, pumpkins and beans on stakes are balanced by rows of greens and herbs.

PREPARATION

Transfer the design to the centre of the linen fabric following the instructions for transferring on page 6.

EMBROIDERY

Cottage outline: one strand of 844 in small backstitches.

Garden seat and wheelbarrow: one strand of 934 in small backstitches.

Watering can and large planter tub: two strands of 934 in satin stitch, with details in backstitch, using one strand of 934.

Cat: two strands of 3799 in satin stitch, with ears, tail and outline in backstitch.

Flowers in large tub: two strands of 3012 in stem stitch for stems; two strands of either 957, 210 or 340 in colonial knots for flowers, mixing the colours at random.

Rose over doorway: two strands of 3012 in stem stitch for stem; two strands of 223 in colonial knots for flowers.

Flowers at doorstep and base of cottage wall: one strand of either ecru, 727 or 320 in colonial knots, ensuring that the green knots remain lower than the ecru and 727. Arrange the knots in groups to resemble clumps of flowers.

Vegetables on left, from top

Rhubarb: two strands of 498 in straight stitches, from a central bottom point, fanning stitches out at the top to form stems, working about five or seven straight stitches for each clump; two strands of 988 in loose lazy daisy stitches to form leaves at the top of stems.

Cauliflower: one strand of ecru in a circular group of colonial knots form the cauliflower head; two strands of 471 in long lazy daisy stitches for leaves around the base of each head, working from the base out and up to the sides.

Silverbeet: two strands of 746 in straight stitch for stems, working in groups of about five stitches for each clump; one strand of 895 in lazy daisy stitch for the leaves on top of stems.

Chives: one strand of 502 in straight stitch for leaves, working each stitch from the base of the row up to the top of the stem and varying the length; one strand of ecru and 340 in colonial knots of alternating colours to form the flowers at the top of the leaves.

Lettuce: two strands of 3348 in bullion stitches (about five bullions) worked in a grub rose formation for the centre of each lettuce; two strands of 988, also in bullion stitches (about four long bullions), for outer leaves.

Runner beans: stitch groups of three stakes, using one strand of 934 and working in backstitch; one strand of 704 for bean stalks, working straight stitches around the stakes and adding colonial knots at the top of stalks.

Pumpkins: two strands of 740 in satin stitch for orange pumpkins, adding highlights with one strand of 924; work one green pumpkin with two strands of 924 only. Stitch vine and leaves with two strands of 988, working in backstitch for stem and satin stitch for leaves.

Seedling row: one strand of 934 for stakes at each end, working in straight stitch; two strands of 370 in a single long floating stitch for the string line. Work seedlings in one strand of 704, stitching two lazy daisy stitches for each seedling. Seed packet on the stake at the right side is stitched with two strands of ecru in satin stitch, with one strand of 704 in lazy daisy stitch over the satin stitch for seedling pictured on seed packet.

Strawberry plants: one strand each of 704 and 988 together in the needle, worked in straight stitch for stems and runners between plants and in lazy daisy stitch for leaves; two strands of 321 in colonial knots for strawberries, placing strawberries below leaves; one strand each of 727 and ecru together in the needle, worked in colonial knots for flowers, placing flowers above leaves.

Pathway: one strand of 919 in backstitch.
Nasturtiums lining pathway: one strand of either 704, 970 or 742 in colonial knots, mixing colours evenly.

COTTAGE LAVENDER SACHET
Filled with dried lavender and shaped to form a cottage, this quick-to-stitch project makes a lovely gift for friends.

11 Cottage Lavender Sachet

MATERIALS

Two 25 cm (10'') squares homespun fabric
DMC six stranded threads in the following colours:
642 beige grey medium, 840 beige brown medium, 610 drab brown very
dark, 355 terracotta dark, 937 avocado green medium, 319 pistachio green
very dark, 335 rose, 791 cornflower blue very dark, 798 delft blue dark,
931 antique blue medium, 350 coral medium, 900 burnt orange dark,
934 black avocado green, 922 copper light, 352 coral light, 3371 black
brown, 987 forest green dark, 725 topaz
Crewel and straw needles
DMC Perle 5 thread: 3348 yellow green light, 3347 yellow green medium
and 352 coral light
Sewing thread
Polyester fibre filling
Dried lavender

Finished size: embroidered area—10 cm x 7 cm (4'' x 2¾'')

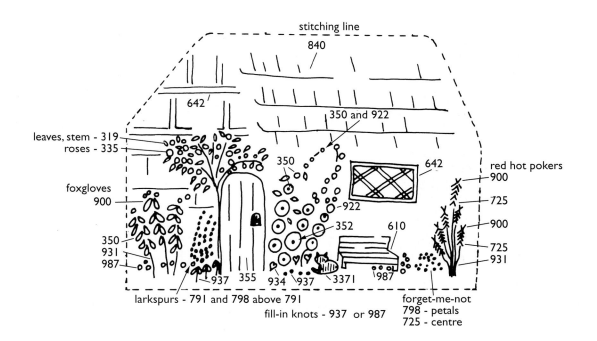

PREPARATION

Transfer the design to the centre of one piece of the homespun following the instructions for transferring on page 6.

EMBROIDERY

Cottage brickwork: one strand of 642 in backstitch.
Roof: one strand of 840 in backstitch for thatch; two strands of 840 in backstitch for outline.
Window: one strand of 642 in backstitch.
Bench: one strand of 610 in backstitch.
Door: one strand 355 in backstitch, with knob in satin stitch.

Flowers at left of door

Roses: one strand of 319 in stem stitch for stem and in lazy daisy stitch for leaves; two strands of 335 in colonial knots for flowers.
Blue larkspurs: one strand of 937 in straight stitch for stems and in lazy daisy stitch for leaves; two strands of 791 in colonial knots for flowers, working from bottom upwards; one strand of 798 in colonial knots for top blooms.
Foxgloves: one strand of 931 in backstitch for stems. Flowers (on left and right): one strand of 350 in lazy daisy stitch, working stitches so they appear to fall down from stem and working two or three colonial knots at top of stalk; (centre stalk): one strand of 900 in lazy daisy stitch and colonial knots as described above for flowers.

Flowers at right of door

Hollyhocks: one strand of 934 in buttonhole stitch for leaves. Flowers (stalk on left): one strand of 350 in buttonhole stitch worked in rounds, gradually becoming smaller towards the top; work a few colonial knots at the top of stalk, using one strand each of 350 and 922 together in the needle; (centre stalk): one strand of 352, with colonial knots at top in one strand of 922; (stalk on right): one strand of 922.
Forget-me-nots: one strand of 798 and 725 in colonial knots, placed between flower stems and below bench to fill gaps.
Red hot pokers: one strand of 931 in stem stitch for stem; one strand of 725 in straight stitch for lower flower petals; one strand of 900 in straight stitch for upper petals.
Green fill-in knots: one strand of 937 or 987 in colonial knots.
Cat: two strands of 3371 in satin stitch, with backstitch outline.

TO MAKE UP

Make a twisted thread cord by twisting a 30 cm (12'') length of each of the three Perle threads together. Pick up the threads in the centre and allow them to twist around each other.

Mark a stitching line around the embroidered cottage. Trim both the embroidered piece and the remaining homespun piece to within 1 cm (½'') of the stitching line. Place the plain homespun piece right sides together with the embroidered piece. Take a 14 cm (5½'') length of the twisted thread cord. Tack one end to each end of the roof. Stitch around the cottage outline, stitching the cord in place and leaving an opening on the bottom edge. Trim the seam and turn pieces right side out. Fill with fibre and dried lavender and stitch the opening closed.

12 Cottage Scene

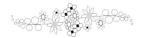

MATERIALS

40 cm x 25 cm (16'' x 10'') piece of homespun fabric
DMC six stranded thread in the following colours:
844 beaver grey ultra dark, 815 garnet medium, 370 beige gold, 975 golden
brown dark, 988 forest green medium, 3801 apricot red, 3807 lavender,
744 yellow pale, 334 baby blue medium, 894 carnation very light, 3815 mid
blue green, 471 avocado green very light, 437 tan light, 321 christmas red,
796 royal blue dark, 746 off white, 890 pistachio green ultra dark,
704 chartreuse bright, 926 light blue green, 3345 hunter green dark,
831 olive green medium
Crewel and straw needles

Finished size: embroidered area—22 cm x 4 cm (9'' x 1½'')

METHOD

Transfer the design to the centre of the homespun following the
instructions for transferring on page 6.

EMBROIDERY

Cottage: one strand of 844 in backstitch.
Door: one strand of 815 in backstitch, with knob in colonial knot.
Fence: two strands of 370 in backstitch.
Birdhouse: one strand of 975 in backstitch.
Flowers around cottage: work all in colonial knots; two strands of 3801,
3807 and 988 for flowers on right of door; one strand of 744, 334, 894

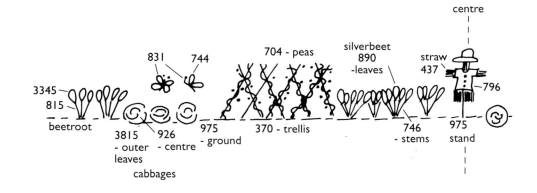

(work in stack for tall flowers) and 3815 for flowers on left of door.
Ground: one strand of 975 in straight stitch.
Scarecrow: one strand of 975 in backstitch for stand; one strand of 437 in satin stitch for straw; one strand of 796 in satin stitch for coat; one strand of 321 in satin stitch for hat and in colonial knots for buttons.
Lettuce: two strands of 471 in bullion stitch for centres; two strands of 988 in bullion stitches worked in a grub rose formation for outer leaves.
Silverbeet: two strands of 746 in straight stitch for stems; one strand of 890 in lazy daisy stitch for leaves.
Peas on trellis: one strand of 370 in backstitch for trellis; one strand of 704 in backstitch for vines and in colonial knots for leaves.
Cabbages: two strands of 926 in bullion stitch for centres; two strands of 3815 in bullion stitches worked in a grub rose formation for outer leaves.
Beetroot: one strand of 815 in straight stitch for stems; one strand of 3345 in lazy daisy stitch for leaves.
Butterflies (left): one strand of 831 for entire butterfly; (right) one strand of 744 for wings and one strand of 831 for body and antennae. Work in lazy daisy stitch for wings, in straight stitch for bodies and in colonial knots for antennae.

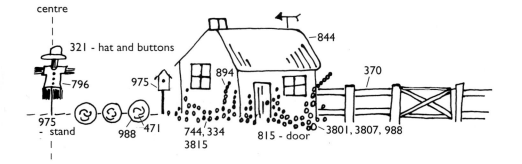

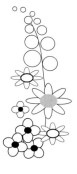

Stitch Guide

BACKSTITCH

BULLION STITCH

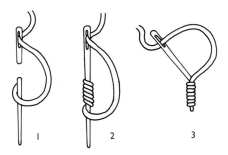

Use a straw or milliner's needle when working bullions. First, take a stitch the same length as the stitch you require. Bring the needle back up at the starting point and leave it in the fabric (1). Wrap the thread around the needle (clockwise for right-handers) 6 to 8 times (or the required number) — (2). Wrap evenly but not firmly. Holding the wraps in place with your finger, pull the needle through, keeping wraps in place and allowing the bullion to fall along the path of the first stitch. Take the needle to the back of the fabric as illustrated (3).

Bullions can be worked as single stitches, placed together in groups or positioned around each other to form a rose shape, see Grub Rose over page.

Work in bullion stitch as described on previous page, placing two or three bullions side by side to form the centre. Then work the next bullion to wrap around one end of the centre. Position the following bullion to wrap around the other end of the centre. Continue to work around the centre, overlapping stitch ends to form a rose shape.

BUTTONHOLE STITCH

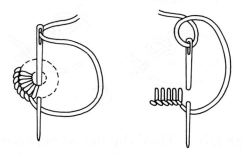

Bring needle through fabric at bottom edge of stitch. Take a downward straight stitch, holding thread under the needle tip. Work from left to right. If working in a circular direction—to form hollyhocks, for example—depending on whether or not you require space in the centre to stitch, either space the centre stitches close together or work from the same point in the centre. If working in a straight line, space stitches parallel and close together.

CHAIN STITCH

Bring needle through the fabric at the top of the position at which you want to form the first stitch. Take a downward stitch, holding the thread

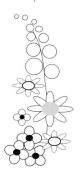

from left to right under the needle tip. Bring the needle through and gently pull the thread to form a chain loop. Continue with the next stitch, which will lock the loop in place. To end the stitching, take the needle back through the fabric below the last loop so that it is held in place.

COLONIAL KNOT

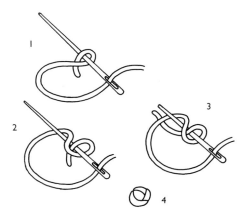

Bring needle through fabric. Hold the thread between your left thumb and index finger (for right-handers). Place the needle under the thread from the left side (1). Pull the thread tight and twist the needle over the top of the thread (2) to form a figure of eight. Insert the needle back through the fabric close to where it emerged (3). Pull the thread then take the needle through the fabric to form the knot (4).

LAZY DAISY STITCH

Bring the needle through the fabric. Hold thread with left hand. Take a downward stitch of the length desired, with thread under needle. Pull needle through, then take a stitch at the bottom of the thread loop, locking loop in place.

RUNNING STITCH

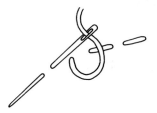

SATIN STITCH

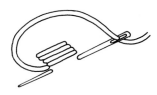

SATIN LEAF STITCH

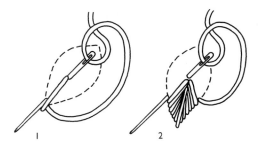

Work from the point of the leaf towards the stem. Start with a straight stitch to form the leaf point. Stitch from the outside edge of the leaf to the centre line, then to the opposite side. Continue to stitch, alternating each side, until leaf is filled.

LONG AND SHORT SATIN STITCH

Work a row of long and short stitches, lining up one end of the stitches with the outline you wish to fill. Then work subsequent rows to fit next to the first row of stitches.

STEM STITCH

STRAIGHT STITCH

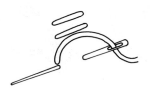

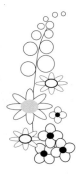